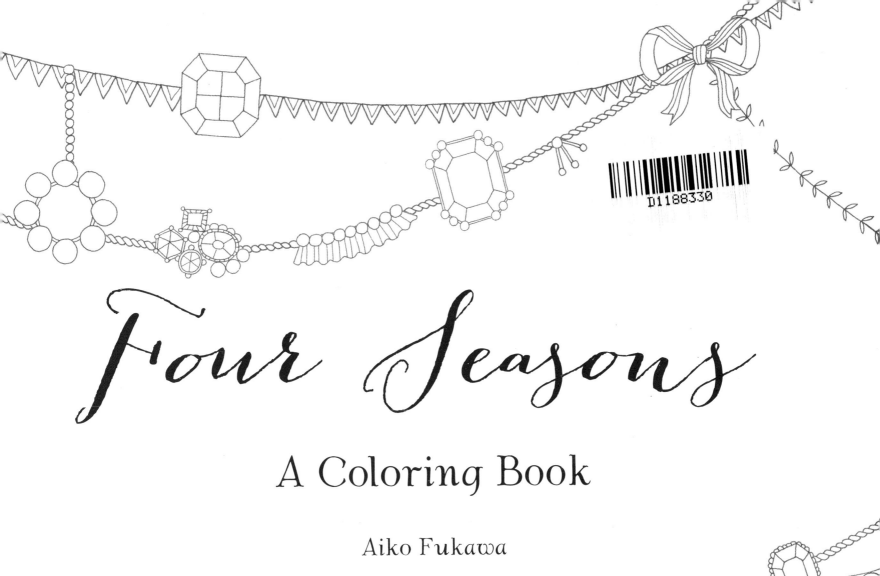

Four Seasons

A Coloring Book

Aiko Fukawa

St. Martin's Griffin
New York

Welcome to the world of four seasons coloring.

Spring to summer, then fall to winter;
as you turn each page the seasons will steadily change.

Motifs involving wonderful flowers and leaves,
or gems and ribbons, are peppered throughout this book.

You can begin coloring anywhere you wish - any page, any color.

A colorful and vibrant universe will emerge
from a world that used to be monochrome.

You are not shackled to descriptions of colors like "an acorn is brown."

Imagine that you are making your own piece of art,
then go ahead and swiftly fill it with colors of your choosing.

Once you finish coloring, you will have created a one-of-a-kind piece of art.

You can use crayons, colored ball-point pens, water-based markers, watercolors,
and of course colored pencils.

Although, it is best not to repeatedly overlay colors
when using water-based markers and watercolors.

If you do happen to overlay colors too many times they will run,
no matter how nice the paper.

A page with pictures printed on translucent paper is
included at the end of this book.

This thin paper will work wonders. By adding color to the pictures under
the translucent paper - and then laying the translucent paper over them -
a whimsical world of color will emerge.

Using materials of your choice,
let's begin coloring the four seasons: spring, summer, fall, and winter.

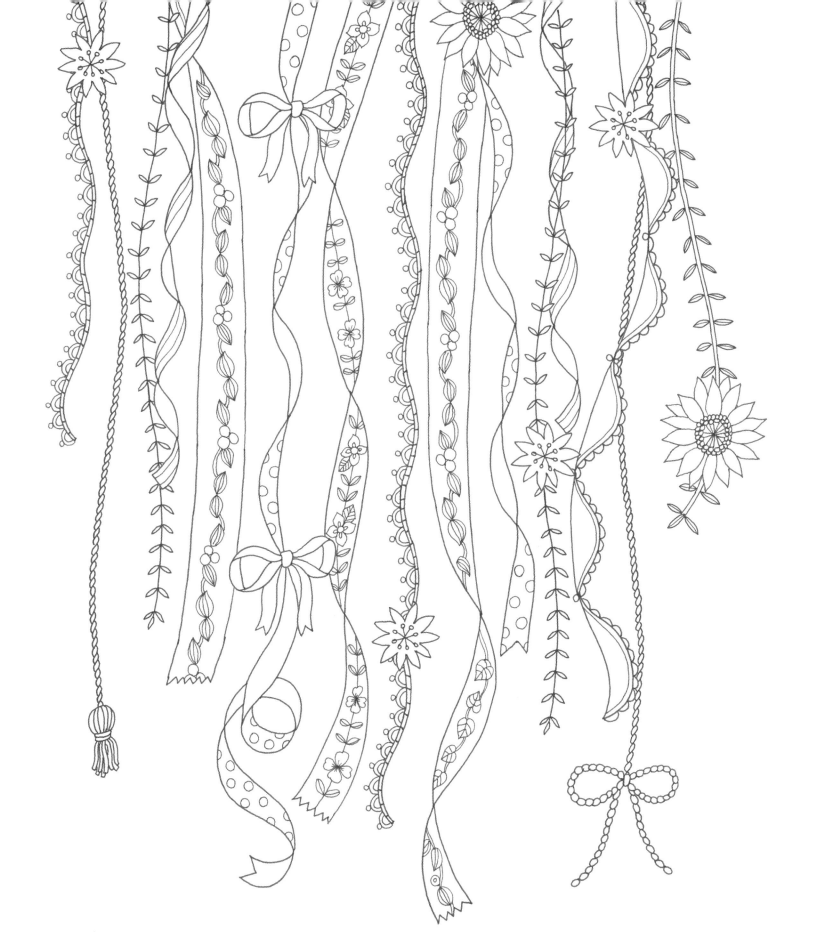

Unlike other pages, this particular page uses a thin translucent paper.

So, you can see everything underneath it, right?

After you color both papers,
lay the translucent page down on top of the other, and together,
they become a beautiful work that differs from the two pages individually.

During my childhood, coloring was one of my favorite activities.

To this day, I still remember the fun of doing nothing but coloring a piece of paper using my favorite colored pencils and crayons.

Once I grew up, there was not much opportunity to color;
but now that I am in charge of illustrations for a coloring book for adults,
my childhood excitement has returned.

Coloring shows a person's individuality. And, depending on your feelings and physical condition on the day you color, the tone of the work will be totally different. I find that very interesting. I honestly think that the colors you choose subconsciously are a manifestation of your mood.

And of course, another attraction to coloring is the actual time you spend doing it
- you are excited, concentrated, and looking forward to finishing while thinking about nothing but selecting the next color to use. You are a little tense when coloring detailed areas... but then, you go on to boldly color larger spaces!
There is an entire drama within a single page.

These concentrated moments are hard to find in daily life,
but coloring allows you to spend quality time with yourself.

As the title Four Seasons implies, motifs related to each of the seasons fill this book. It is fun to color while imagining scenery and memories from every time of the year. Although, I should say that coloring freely and intuitively can also be fun.
Any style is okay really, it's your call!

Finally, when you finish coloring this entire book it will become your own one-of-a-kind collection of artwork. Each and every page will make you feel a multitude of emotions and think various thoughts, even though no words are used.

I really hope you have a great time with your own Four Seasons.

Aiko Fukawa

Aiko Fukawa Profile

An illustrator and designer of the paper art "ai" brand.
Graduated from Tokyo University of Arts, Department of Design in 2005.
Fukawa has been actively involved with projects in advertising,
book cover design, stationery, magazines, and picture books.
Also, Fukawa has held private exhibitions internationally
and worked on projects for overseas clients
such as FLOW, the Dutch magazine.

Four Seasons
by Aiko Fukawa

First designed and published in Japan in 2014
by Graphic-sha Publishing Co., Ltd.
1-14-17 Kudankita, Chiyoda-ku, Tokyo 102-0073, Japan
Copyright © 2014 Aiko Fukawa
Copyright © 2014 Graphic-sha Publishing Co., Ltd.

English text copyright © 2015 St. Martin's Press.
For information, address 175 Fifth Avenue, New York, N.Y. 10010.

www.stmartins.com

ISBN 978-1-250-08262-6

St. Martin's Griffin books may be purchased for educational, business, or promotional use. For information on bulk
purchases, please contact the Macmillan Corporate and Premium Sales Department at 1-800-221-7945, extension 5442, or
write to specialmarkets@macmillan.com.

First U.S. Edition: September 2015

10 9 8 7 6 5 4 3

Creative staff
Author: Aiko Fukawa
Planning and editing: Junko Tsuda (Graphic-sha Publishing Co., Ltd.)
Book design: Naoko Nakui

English edition
English translation: Kevin Wilson
English edition layout: Shinichi Ishioka

Production and management: Kumiko Sakamoto
                            (Graphic-sha Publishing Co., Ltd.)

This edition was coordinated by LibriSource Inc.

Printed and bound in China